JUSTIN
GROWING THROUGH THE PAIN OF LOSS

I0177101

IJEOMA OLISA

SYNCTERFACE™
Syncterface Media
London
syncterfacemedia.com

JUSTIN

GROWING THROUGH THE PAIN OF LOSS

ISBN: 978-1-912896-01-1
Copyright © October 2018 by Ijeoma Olisa
All Rights Reserved

Published in the United Kingdom by

SYNCTERFACE™

Syncterface Media
London

www.syncterfacemedia.com
info@syncterfacemedia.com

Cover Design:
Syncterface Media, London

This book is printed on acid-free paper

Dedication

To our charming *Chukwuka 'Justin' Olisa* – our angel in heaven. A bright light, as brief as it may have been, that shone through our home and hearts.

&

To every parent who has lost a child, this is for you.

Acknowledgements

To God Almighty, I thank you for sending amazing people my way who walked this journey with me.

My dearest FrancoNero, I love you. We have walked this path together with our beautiful children Nnoye, Dumebi & Debe. God bless you all.

My Parents – Sir and Lady Umezuruike, my mother-in-law – Mrs Franca Olisa, my ever supportive sisters-in-law, my Sister Chii & her hubby Nicky. You are all amazing.

House On The Rock, my family forever. There are so many of you all over the world that just do not stop checking.

The Watchers – if I did not learn to pray, my mind would have been totally messed up. To every Watcher Sister out there who has been a part of this journey, even though we have not met physically. God bless you.

Akin Akinyemi – you made this come alive just because you believed in me. There are no words……. Thank you!

Contents

Comments on Justin

Pain is pain in every language & only God knows how to hold us up when our world seems to be falling apart. Our God truly makes absolutely all things work together for our good...even our greatest pains.

Through the misery of grief, I know God has granted you a ministry to minister to the grieving, especially those who have suffered "sudden" loss of a loved one.

Justin is irreplaceable but through this book, his legacy and ministry shall live on!

I know the grief of a mother is unique to the rest of the family as the baby was in your womb before the world knew and from the same womb Heaven has blessed you to birth this book.

May all who have suffered similar loss find purpose, encouragement, direction, divine sense and meaning in the none sense of human grief.

We laugh death to scorn when we look at the bigger picture because time is just a bleep in eternity and as believers in Christ, we know the story is not over. Soon we shall know no grief and be with our Lord and loved ones forever.

God bless you for the courage to allow yourself be a source of strength to others. Let the healing waters flow over every soul that reads this book and may the same waters heal your soul.

~ **Pastor Jim Bent** ~
House On The Rock, South Africa

I started reading this book and found it so captivating that I could not stop until I finished reading. I believe that God will heal so many hurting from, not just the loss of a child but from any form of loss through this book.

I remember desperately looking for a book to recommend when Justin passed. I wanted you to hear what someone who had walked the same path as you had to say but found none. Now there is a book of comfort from someone who has been there and knows exactly how it hurts to lose a child.

May God bless you for yielding yourself as an instrument in God's hand to touch hurting people. This is indeed His purpose that we comfort others with the same comfort we have received from him.

Hmmm...it takes courage for you to have done this. You have risen from the pit the enemy intended to keep you; from ashes and sackcloth to the place of glory.

~ **Pastor Jumoke Bent** ~
House On The Rock, South Africa

It is tough to remain thankful when life throws curveballs at us, and it seems we have lost the very essence of what we live for. Yet in moments of deep hurt and loss, Ijeoma dares to turn these for the good of others and to focus on a higher purpose. I commend your courage and generosity.

Justin's brief life on earth has left an indelible mark on us; Chukwuka is now our angel and saint. His memory lives on, for God is truly the Greatest.

~ **NsimaAgnes** ~
Justin's Birthday Mate

Chuka my friend, my playmate, my jolly happy son that could scatter for Africa and still be happy and laughing while at it.

We didn't expect your coming but very happy that you came. You brought peace, joy and so much fun. I wish I knew your stay was but for a little while, I would have hugged and played with you more and allowed you to scatter more of my stuff.

I so cherish the two weeks I spent with you. Rest on little Angel and keep smiling in heaven.

~ **Pastor Ama Bassey-Fynch** ~
House On The Rock, Lagos

<u>1</u>

A Word from the Author

*T*ime, they say heals wounds. I wish I could boldly say that for myself. Time has not been friendly with me or should I say, my case is just different? These were the kind of thoughts that came through my mind as I struggled with the challenge I now had to overcome. The battle in my mind was more vicious than I could ever have conceived.

Emerging from the dark night of intense storms, I knew I had to find purpose in these events, I had to find a way to help others who may have found themselves in a similar situation to mine.

What better way than to tell my story.

The prompt to write

The desire to write my story is not something I had thought about, it sort of came upon me suddenly. It was on Saturday 22nd October 2016, as I sat in

Church, I shared a photo of Justin which he took with Pastor Dare Oluwasanmi's cap with him and the memories came flooding back and Pastor Dare asked me a simple question – "Have you ever thought of writing about your experience, writing a book to share your story?" Obviously, I had never considered writing, I mean… I'm not an author, what do I know about writing?

Truth be told, a few years back I had desired to write a series of short stories but I never quite went beyond the first few pages. So yes, for a few minutes I thought through that conversation. Then by the time the service was done, after returning to his chair, the guest speaker, Mr. Fela Durotoye, came back and said God asked him to impart someone in the hall who had a book inside of them to write. I knew at that moment that it was time to tell my story. I walked out and received the blessing.

After receiving the blessing, I was confused about what to do with the gift that had been given for me to write. I had to run to the one person who I knew would be able to help me, my friend of many years - Akin Akinyemi. I called him and we spoke for a long time. He took me through step by step of how to take seriously the impartation that I had received from Mr. Fela Durotoye and how I should just write a few words a day, a paragraph a day, a page a day.

"Just write something every day" Akin said. "And always remember we are here for you" he reassured.

In pursuit of purpose

As I thought about the experiences of my life, a scripture came to my mind that helped me realise a lot more could be achieved in Justin's absence than in his presence depending on which outcome I chose to live with.

> [30]*"Then Samson said, 'Let me die with the Philistines!' And he pushed with all his might and the temple fell on the lords and all the people who were in it. So the dead that he killed at his death were more than he had killed in his life"*
>
> *Judges 16:30*

"How?" was my next question.

There were so many questions running through my mind but I made up my mind to do something that will bless other children: maybe set up a foundation, send a child to school, feed a child, give another child a glimpse of the heaven that my Justin is in now.

"His death has to count for something." I thought to myself.

Having a part of me in South African soil had to count for something. I knew there must be a way for me to grow from this suffocating pain.

I have seen myself grow from someone who was speechless when there was a death, to someone who just knows how to be there for the bereaved. I have learned to be there for the person who has lost a business or lost a marriage.

A loss is a loss. For me, it was my baby, for another it may be a spouse, yet again a parent, a sibling, a dream or a business. That comfort I was running away from, I now understand that the God of all comforts is always there to comfort us in His own way, we only need to let Him know where it hurts.

So that's how we got to this point, I will share my story. I will be there to cry with any other person hurting in a similar way. It's ok to cry, it's ok to ask questions, it's even ok to get angry. But at the end of the day, our trust in God must remain resolute and unshaken because He rules and reigns in the affairs of men.

2

Such a Dark Night

*I*n the past year, I have felt pain so deep, I could touch or hold it. Pain that makes breathing difficult, pain that makes you feel like you're suffocating, pain that won't just go away. However, I have chosen to turn this pain to my gain. I will like to share the journey of that pain and how it has transformed and still is transforming my life.

Saturday 21st November 2015, my family and I got up to the dawning of a new day. We thanked God for the gift of life and the privilege of living then continued with our normal routine for the day. I was out for a meeting that day and when I got back home, my dear Justin ran across the parking lot to give me a 'Welcome home mommy' hug. We went in together and after I settled down, I continued with the work that was pending while Justin sat on my laps as I punched away on my laptop.

Suddenly, he felt sick and started to throw up. I

stopped temporarily to clean him up and continued with my work.

In the meantime, whatever he threw up smelt vile so I asked questions: "What did he eat? Where did he go? What happened?" These questions seemed rhetorical because there were no answers out of the ordinary so life went on. He threw up a couple more times and stopped. So I felt all was well.

I had to go to church for a conference so I left the kids at home with my mom. I made a few calls to get an update on his health so I recommended a couple of home remedies.

This was my fourth child, "surely we could handle day 1 of diarrhoea." I thought. By the time I got home later that night, he had started stooling. I became very concerned that I did not sleep through that night. I just watched over him and waited for the morning sun so I could get to the nearest pharmacy to re-stock on medications.

In the morning, my husband left for church with the other kids while I promised to join them later after sorting Mr. Justin out. My initial plan was to go by a pharmacy, get some more medication and head on to church. But very much unlike me, I decided to go with him to the clinic and get a proper prescription so my mom insisted she would go with me. When I got to the first clinic, his temperature was already very high, the doctor checked his vitals while the nurses administered a pain-killer, then we were referred to the hospital.

Armed with my referral in hand I drove like a mad

woman to the hospital straight to the ER (Emergency Room). The medical team proceeded to check his vitals, something was wrong, he was put on a drip and admitted.

"For diarrhoea?" I questioned. Then there were more doctors, questions were asked: Had he had all his immunizations? Had he travelled to Nigeria recently? (This was during the Ebola scare), How long had he been stooling and throwing up? And many more questions.

He had started to get cold so he was placed under some heat. He was later moved to another bed. I looked at my son and he was just so weak. He kept asking me for 'Sar' (his own little way of calling water) and yes I gave him water. I would have given him anything he asked for just for the pain to go away. More machines were brought to check his heart rate and other vitals, checks were done, the doctors were discussing the 'strange' results, everything was blurry to me.

During this saga, my husband was still at church with the older kids, I tried to reach him but that was almost impossible. Eventually I got through to him through someone else and he came through to the hospital to find out what was happening while the older kids went home with pastor's family.

I was so glad my husband got to the hospital just in time; little did we know we were on a timer which was on a fast count-down.

I sat by him, rubbing his hands and body to soothe him and keep him warm. Suddenly, his breathing got very fast and stopped. Unable to believe what happened and contain my shock, I took a closer look.

"No! It can't be!!!" I thought to myself, I called his name – "Chuka, Chukwuka, Justin, do you want water? Chuu". I asked frantically. He did not answer me, he was still.

3

Slipped Into Eternity

I shouted for the doctor, she came in, took one look at him and ushered me out. My Husband came back into the room and asked what was happening. I was not coherent

"He he he was breathing," I stuttered,

"He was talking to me," I shook as I narrated what happened.

"Then he started to breathe so fast and stopped." I concluded, refusing to accept what just happened.

"What was happening?" I was confused.

His bed had been cordoned off; all the doctors and nurses surrounded his bed, the lead doctor shouted all sorts of orders and then there were more machines.

I sent messages out to every prayer group I belonged to, I called my brother in-law, Nick, who is a pastor.

"Today is a Sunday, surely God would hear one of the prayers raised," I said. Everyone prayed. I quoted every scripture I remembered.

The doctor came through and wanted to talk, I knew my baby was gone but I refused to listen. I instructed that no one should touch my son, my baby.

"Don't touch him!" I yelled.

"Don't take him away from here, God will come through." I begged.

"I have to wait for my pastor, just leave him there." I pleaded.

I cried some more, prayed some more and just refused to look at his lifeless body. My pastors got there and prayed and oh we prayed. My son lay there for hours while I refused for the death certificate to be issued or for his body to be taken to a morgue.

Finally, I had to release him because it was clear that heaven had received him and he was glad to step into glory.

"Did he really choose to leave his mom?" I asked.

"Did he not see I was hurting?" I wondered.

The tears flowed freely and I did not hold back. And so that night, I walked away from the hospital, leaving the lifeless body of my son on that bed wondering where I had gone wrong or who I had offended. None of it made any sense.

Looking at him, he looked, oh so peaceful, and beautiful, even in death he had that endearing smile still plastered on his face. How was it then possible that this lovely child who looked like he was asleep had actually slipped into eternity?

4

Justin Has Gone Home

My husband, my mom and I got home so broken. Our pastors stayed a while with us. I could only send one message to my friend and neighbour – "*Your Justin has gone home to be with his maker.*" A few people came around that night and we all cried together. When everyone left we tried to eat, considering no one had eaten all day and we all slept in the living room with just a little bit of hope in our hearts that this was all a bad joke.

A major light in my life had just been turned off. What a dark night it really was!

This makes me think of the night God gave up His only son. *Luke 23:45 "And the sun was darkened, and the veil of the temple was rent in the midst"*

If God felt dark the day His son laid down His life then surely the darkness I felt that day was ok.

I tried to preach to myself saying it could not have

been easy for the Father to give up His son for a world that really did not deserve it. We continued in sin, yet He gave up His only son for you and I. He turned his back on His only son, forsaking Him at that point when all the sin of the world was on Him because our God cannot behold sin.

As much as He loved His son, He just could not look upon Him. Turning away from your child is the most heart-wrenching, heart-breaking thing to do.

But hey, at one point or the other just like with God our Father and His son Jesus Christ, there are some journeys we cannot go on with our children, they just have to walk alone.

5

The News

*L*et's take a break and let me take you back to the beginning of this walk.

It was in May, 2013. We had been in South Africa for just about a year then. Things had gone from bad to worse and still no ray of hope, no indication that the difficulties were ending soon. I was just rounding off the short course I had registered for at the University of South Africa and our marriage was really rocky. It was getting to the point where I really was upset that we had to suffer so much. I sought counsel and what came through was not to deny hubby his rights, especially in the bedroom and really at that point I knew I was guilty and so I decided to have a make-up session, fully protected by the way.

Few weeks down the line I started to feel funny, knowing my body as well as I did I knew I was pregnant.

"What?" I was shocked.

"When we could hardly feed ourselves and the three kids we already had? How?" I asked myself.

We had closed shop, we wanted to have three kids and we already had the three, a good mix of two girls and a boy. I was so angry! I blamed my husband for getting me pregnant. I blamed God for by-passing the many couples that had been married long years without a child of their own.

"How could He give this child to a family that was already fully booked?" I questioned.

My fitness streak kicked in. Every morning when I was left alone I would put on the tightest girdle I had and do a hundred sit ups with the hope that it would sort of 'dislodge' the baby and I would not be guilty of getting rid of the child but the baby kept growing and getting stronger.

I missed Church for the first time in my life because I really felt cheated.

"Why serve a God who would give me what I did not need?" I asked.

"I needed a job, more money, not a baby." My thoughts screamed at me.

Then, phone calls came through, while some people asked what I was thinking to get myself pregnant when I could hardly feed my family, some others were very happy at the prospect of another member of the family. Yet some others had words of prophecy saying this was the child of promise bringing a lot of turn around.

The one call that made a big difference for me was the call from my dad. He referred me to Job Chapters 38 and 39 where God finally spoke to Job with many questions. This chapter sort of became the hallmark of my life and the baby growing in my womb. It revealed to me the supremacy of God in everything. I realised I was just a mere man, unable to determine the outcome of life. This is God who turns blood into a child:

"Wow, for one woman the same blood comes out as a menstrual period while for another woman the blood is formed into a baby." I mused.

I am not a medical doctor so I am not going to even try explaining the process of conception, but as a woman I know that on months when it's not a baby, then it's blood. I repented and bowed down before God, the creator of all things.

In the midst of all these, God gave me the names of the child – Justin Chukwuka. I checked the meaning of Justin, considering I did not even know anyone called Justin. Justin means "Just, Upright, Righteous"; Chukwuka means "God is the greatest".

God spoke to me in a still quiet voice; "Nothing can stop me from being God. In everything that I do I am just, my ways are always righteous, I can justify every situation that I take you through, over and above all I am the greatest, greater than this pregnancy, greater than your financial situation, greater than the scientists that invented family planning and all sorts of protection, greater than life itself". And so it kept ringing in my head "God is the greatest and He is justified in everything that I go through."

By the way I never carried out a scan to check the sex of my babies, all four of them. I like the element of surprise. This however was the first child that we had a name for from the first trimester. Many times I tried to get female options, just in case a girl popped out, but I was as blank as could be. This had never happened before. And so I boldly told hubby the names and we agreed. This made prayer during the pregnancy easier because as was hubby's ritual, he would lay hands on my tummy every day and pray for the baby, the difference is that this time he would be able to call the name of the child and pray.

We prepared to receive our baby. We knew him by name even before he manifested.

God knows you by name. Isaiah 43: 1 "But now, thus saith the Lord that created thee, O Jacob, and he that formed thee, O Israel, fear not: for I have redeemed thee, I have called thee by name; thou art mine"

No one wants to relate with a stranger or with someone who does not know you by name. We are always more endeared to that person who always calls us by name.

Now, the creator of the universe says He knows you by name; you are not just an afterthought. He prepared a space for you on this earth, God deliberately sent you to your family, He intentionally made you a man or a woman, He was convinced when he made you light skinned or dark skinned.

God has always been full of purpose regarding you, nothing is a mistake. So really, we should not be afraid because He was always intentional concerning our design.

6

Planning For Justin

All through the pregnancy, we made a lot of plans. I started to save a bit; I identified things we could buy for the baby, where he would sleep, how we would take care of him. My third child was 5 years old at the time so really I had almost forgotten how to take care of a new baby but we're women, it always comes back.

Just before Justin

All of my pre-natal visits happened at the primary health care centre just by the house but on my last visit we had been told where the delivery would happen. Hubby and I took a drive down to identify the clinic. We went in and asked the relevant questions to know what to do when labour actually kicked in. With all questions asked, we were armed with all the information we needed to receive dear baby Justin.

At this time I was working at the House on the Rock church office, so I continued to work for as long as I had the energy to move myself. I tried to take long walks with hubby just to keep myself active and make sure the baby did not get lazy (as our people back home would say).

We had sent word back home on the Expected Date of Delivery, so my mother made plans to visit South Africa for the first time so she could assist with the baby post-delivery. I had made my list of every delicacy I wanted to have from home as a nursing mother. All plans were in place.

This takes me back to how God our Father planned for the world to receive His son for the salvation and redemption of the world. He started by first sending the patriarchs (Abraham, Isaac, Jacob); then He sent the prophets, major and minor (Isaiah, Jeremiah, Nahum…). There were sacrifices of bull, sheep, doves and much more but these could only cover the sin of man for a limited period.

Then God decided to send His son. From time he planned adequately to ensure the world was prepared to receive His son. The prophets announced it many years before Christ was born.

The angels announced it to Mary and Joseph was told in a dream.

Elizabeth was told and her son, the child of her old age was sent specifically to be a fore runner to announce the Son of God that takes away the sin of the world.

It is always important to plan with precision just like God our Father. Not just for the birth of a baby, but even for the birth of a business, a dream. Anything you are giving life to requires diligent planning and preparation.

The arrival of Justin

Early on January 18th 2014, I started to feel very uneasy and so I knew that at the break of dawn we would head to the clinic. We packed the baby bag, dropped the kids off with friends and headed off to the clinic. The necessary checks were done and I was admitted.

Labour is never easy, the pain would come and go and I had to bear it all. I tried to distract myself by staying on my phone as much as possible; I walked up and down the corridors until the pain peaked. There were some more checks and I was ushered into the delivery room.

For the first time in all four baby deliveries, hubby was allowed into the room. The other three were born back home in Nigeria and for some reason my doctor did not just allow the men in. The nurses attended to me and in practically just one push I heard hubby say "Hey, Justin is here!" then I knew that truly I had birthed the promised son.

While I was being cleaned, I was made to carry him for one hour making him latch on to my nipple and try to feed. It was only after this that I was taken out of the delivery room to the post-natal ward. My baby was taken away, cleaned, properly dressed and brought back to me. We were observed for some time and then discharged the same day.

It felt good to be home the same day as I really did not look forward to sleeping at the clinic that night. The kids were beside themselves to have their baby brother home. He was given his first bath with the help of Pastor Jumoke and Yemisi. We settled into our new life with baby Justin quite fast I must say.

For the first time I did not have my usual combo of my mom and mom-in-law to help. I was alone. Mom was due to be in South Africa (SA) in a few days. I had help from my church family and definitely from hubby, so it made it easier. How could it be that after all the planning I still had to be by myself for some days before help arrived? Hmm, life happens. Anyway, this helped us – my husband, the three older kids and I to get closer, taking care of the baby and his immediate needs without having to share with anyone else.

> *"And she brought forth her firstborn son, and wrapped him in swaddling clothes, and laid him in a manger; because there was no room for them in the inn."*
>
> *Luke 2: 7*

I reflected on how Mary had to give birth to her son in similar conditions, in a strange land because they had travelled from Nazareth to Bethlehem to be counted. There was no room and so she had her baby in a manger. How humbling, that the saviour of the world was born in a manger.

This was definitely part of God's plan, after all, He had always known that His son would be born at that time; He had always known that the census would happen at that time when His son would be born. Why did He not make it possible for Joseph to secure a room for the birth of His son? Better still, why did He not make it possible for them to have returned home, to Mary's place of safety and birth the Son of God in Nazareth?

It was all part of the plan.

7

Living with Justin

*L*iving life with Justin was such a delight. He grew up as a healthy child; started crèche at an early age and God connected us to a divine lady called Ingrid who took very good care of Justin that we eventually moved our older son from his former crèche to the same crèche as Justin's. The boys just loved to be at school together.

Every morning, Justin loved to be given a bath by his father and without fail my husband gave him a bath with his brother (that was the daily routine). He would bath him and I would dress him up. If anyone else tried to give him a bath there will be war in the house that morning. We would then drop off the girls at big school, then take the boys to their own 'little school'. Justin was not a fussy baby, he ate very well, was not sickly at all, he had all his immunizations done and even on days when he would get multiple injections he would not have a fever.

My Justin just loved to dance, he would stay up late with me watching TV and dancing to every song danceable.

He did not miss the morning devotions at home especially the praise and worship when he would clap and dance even when he could not sing the songs.

He was truly the fairest of all four; people who met him fell in love with him instantly. Those who had not met him and just saw his photos absolutely loved him and looked forward to meeting him. He was certainly a charmer.

Don't get me wrong, I love all my children – each one unique in their own way but this particular son of mine was different and very handsome. At a point, a naughty friend of mine requested that I had a maternity test done to be sure my baby was not swapped at the clinic and I told her then that my confidence was that I was the only one at the clinic on the day I gave birth to Justin.

He was a unifier that brought everyone in the house together.

He shadowed his brother Debe so well, he followed his every footstep and of course his big brother was too glad that he had someone to teach.

Nnoye, our first, took such special care of him and Dumebi was finally glad that there was an even split in the house – two girls and two boys, so the lines could be drawn evenly.

Our Justin was such an easy baby; the pregnancy

was great, I was not sick at all. He fed very well, no colic, slept long hours at night. Did not hassle any nanny, or if I had to drop him off at the neighbours there was never any issue. Once he had been given a bottle and noodles, he was good to go.

As is the tradition in the house, we celebrated his first birthday with a pool party and it was quite grand. I am sure he had a lot of fun even though we all know that all these first birthdays are more for the adults and older kids than actually for the celebrant.

He was my prayer partner because somewhere along the way, I signed on to The Watchers, a group of women who keep watch over their homes, children and community. I was learning to pray with a purpose.

At a point, I determined to keep the first watch of the day which I figured from some personal study, was about 3am. My Justin would wake me up, without fail, at 10 minutes to 3am daily to make a bottle for him and so since I was awake at the time I would pray. He would stay with me until I was done then we would go in together and sleep till morning.

He was a very fast learner, picking up so much from school and from his siblings, learning to talk fast and calling each person by name at home.

> [52]*And Jesus increased in wisdom and stature, and in favour with God and man.*"
>
> *Luke 2: 52*

Being the son of God did not mean an automatic growth for Jesus, it was still incremental. It is always joyful watching a child grow and pick certain values that your household is known for. It must have brought much joy to God the Father, watching His son increase.

We have the blessings of God over our lives but if we do not truly apply ourselves, growth will not come through. As parents we have to make a deliberate effort to teach our children the right things from a tender age. They never forget what they have been taught from a heart of love.

> [6] *Start off children on the way they should go, and even when they are old they will not turn from it.*
>
> Proverbs 22: 6 (NIV)

Looking back now, I realise that many things that I was afraid of became non-issues. For instance, when I conceived Justin, I walked into the mall and just looking at the cost of diapers, baby food, clothes and all that made me cry. I did not know how we would afford to take care of a baby. Everything was just too expensive. Up till this moment, I cannot tell you how we took care of Justin all those years but he never lacked food, clothes, diapers, he was well taken care of by God. It seemed like the raven that God sent to cater for Prophet Elijah was living right in my house.

8

The Immediate Aftermath

*N*ow I'm back to Sunday 22nd November 2015. Unknown to me, while Justin was making his transition at the hospital and others were at church, there was a child (Yaddah), a few weeks younger than my Justin, who was just misbehaving in church. One of the ladies at church called hubby and asked him to check on that boy and from the minute he saw hubby he just clung onto him, refusing to let go for the rest of the service.

Everyone wondered what was happening. When I heard that story, it made me realise the strength of spirit that even children under the age of two had a bond between brothers from different mothers.

His mom and I shared the season of pregnancy together, comparing notes. In September of 2015 they had need to sleep over at ours, immediately the two boys saw themselves, they hugged like their lives depended on it; "Young 'unintelligent' boys?

What did they really know?" the mothers exchanged glances.

So yeah, it made me realise that there is truly a spirit in man that is ageless. Job 32: 8-9 "But there is a spirit in man, and the breath of the Almighty gives him understanding. Great men are not always wise, nor do the aged always understand justice."

Our spirit is the same age from birth to death just that as our body matures, our spirit gets expression. As we learn to know God and become born again, our spirit is regenerated. When our bodies die and our spirit steps into eternity, we are not old and haggard in heaven. It's the same spirits, just different levels of expression as our bodies mature. This is what I have come to believe over time.

The house was full of people, the calls never stopped coming through, WhatsApp messages, text messages, Blackberry messages, and we were truly overwhelmed. Many people called crying on the phone for a child they had never met. All this while, our older kids were still at Pastor Bent's house with Nnoye calling every hour to find out how their brother was doing, if he was better, when they could come home?

Really, hubby and I were not ready to break the news. We did not know what to say to them, how to say it to them, could not imagine how they would react.

Our older daughter, Nnoye, was writing term exams at school so we had the dilemma of deciding how to tell the kids that their baby brother was no more.

They had spent the night at Pastor's place. We sent their school uniforms to them so they could go to school on Monday 23rd November.

We had gone to the school to speak with a counsellor and find out what effect this death could have on her grades for the school year. It was such a big relief to know that she had a choice to write her exams earlier so that the news could be broken to her; and even if she decided not to write, she still had grades strong enough to get her a promotion to the next year. Having this knowledge we made the decision to let the kids know.

We prayed for strength to make it down to the home of the Bents where our older children were. It was the most difficult thing to explain to them that Justin was no more a sojourn on this earth. At ages 10 and 8, the girls got it but it took our 6 year old Debe moments to understand what was happening.

"Do you mean we will not see Justin again?"Debe asked.

It hurt my heart so much to give answers to such questions. For years we had preached to them how Jesus healed the sick and raised the dead, they wanted to know why their own sick was not healed and why their own dead was not raised. They wondered how come it was not only old people that died. Even though we did not have all the answers at that moment, we assured them of God's love and the truth that Justin was now in a better place.

The girls were strong, they continued to go to school, but my Debe, oh dear he was so broken, he refused to go back to the school he shared with his brother.

Few months earlier, in June 2015, we had secured admission for him to move to big school with his sisters but when we told him, he refused because he wanted to remain at the creche.

We did not bother much because he was due to resume in January 2016 so there was still time enough to convince him to change school. At this point however, he was so ready to move to his new school as it was clear that one more day at his old school without his brother would not happen.

> [11]*The race is not to the swift, Nor the battle to the strong, Not bread to the wise, nor riches to men of understanding, nor favour to men of skill; But time and chance happen to them all.*
>
> *Ecclesiastes 9:11*

Truly, at this point, I realised that it was not about how convincing we were to get Debe to change schools because we had tried and failed. It was not about how swift our speech was or how intelligent our argument was, God had to do His work at His own time. Truly this was the right time for Debe to embrace the move to a new school.

Justin's death strongly impacted the kids, and a few days later Debe got ill. It started with a sore throat then an inflamed lymph node at the back of his neck. His neck became misaligned that, even when he was walking straight, his head was looking sideways. He was also not responding to treatment.

We took him to the clinic and after a couple of

background checks, not finding anything wrong with him, the doctor asked more psychological questions, wanting to know if he had been in any recent trauma.

At that point we realised that he was dealing with the loss in his own way. This was a scary period, watching our older son take ill and not respond to treatment. This was a bit too much to bear. We ran to God and asked him to heal and yes, He came through for us.

> [9] *"What do you conspire against the Lord? He will make an utter end of it. Affliction will not rise up a second time."*
>
> *Nahum 1:9*

When I had no other scripture to quote, I begged God to take away the affliction of watching another sick child taken away from me; I really could not deal with it.

School resumed in January; I made a decision to take the names of all the teachers in which classes my children were and I prayed for favour.

> [15] *Now when the turn came for Esther the daughter of Abihail, the uncle of Mordecai, who had taken her as his daughter, to go in to the king, she requested nothing but what Hegai the king's eunuch, the custodian of the women, advised. And Esther obtained favour in the sight of all who saw her.*
>
> *Esther 2:15*

I spent many days declaring a new level of favour on the children. Favour from colleagues, from teachers, from authorities. Just favour.

At first Debe struggled with his school work and we did not just understand what was happening. I had to let his teacher know that we were going through a transitional season.

God just gave us the perfect teacher for this school year. She understood our situation and worked with us to help settle Debe into the new school year, she even got him to talk about the loss of his baby brother and how it affected him. I believe that was when his healing started. God was truly faithful to us every step of the way.

We are not there yet, but we've certainly made a lot of progress. There have been days when the children just cry because they remember their brother and all I can tell them is that we will all be fine.

Yes I believe that we will all be fine, I don't know when but surely we will be fine.

My dear FrancoNero

In these days, I came to see and appreciate the strength and resilience of my dear "FrancoNero."

Hubby remained firm in all he had to do. He did not miss a day of praying in the morning even when it hurt so much and he had to pray alone.

Those mornings I did not want to get up from bed because of the magnanimity of the pain, he would lead us all in prayer consistently. He kept the fort and kept the household together.

He had days when he would just break down and

cry, really cry because the one child who made him look forward to coming home every day was no longer there to run to the door and welcome him.

Of course the other kids love him very much but they're all gone past that age of running to the door to welcome "Daddy Dadaa".

In Franco's words, "*I miss Justin so much, I miss all the times when I come back home from a very hectic day at work and once I come through the door I hear him hail me "Daddy Dadaa" and he gives me a hug and all the weariness in me just melts away.*

I miss all those times he comes and imposes himself between myself and my wife on the bed as if he is telling us that is his space, I miss his smile cos it lights up the place.

I miss when I take him to school and he always insists on dragging his elder brother's stroller bag instead of his and marches majestically to his class and dropping off the bag in the right place.

I choose to believe that his "Daddy Dadaa" means good father, I thank God that though his stay on this earth was short, it was very impactful and I cherish every moment he spent with us to the glory of God."

9

When Reality Bites

I n the days following the transition of our dear Justin, the house was always full. Different people brought in food, flowers, candles were lit, and his photos were in the house. It was all about Justin.

The Funeral

The funeral date was fixed for Friday, 27th November 2015. The undertakers had gone to prepare his body and made all the arrangements to get the body to the cemetery; my husband certainly had a lot of running around to do.

My sister arrived our place the night before. It really felt great to have the sort of support that I had. My House on the Rock church family was there too. People actually left work to be there to celebrate the life and times of little Mr. Justin.

There was a small service by the grave side, we got

to see him one last time just before the service kicked off. He looked so resplendent in the 3-piece suit Clarrise had bought for him a few months earlier. My older kids were so strong throughout the service.

Then his body was committed to mother earth, I think that was another very heart-wrenching moment, leaving that body in the casket underneath all of that soil.

Months after that, I definitely struggled to stay behind closed doors because I felt suffocated. I have never been claustrophobic in my life, but in those moments I always felt suffocated each time I thought of the fact that I left my son alone in a morgue and in the soil.

Truth be told, of course I knew that was not my son anymore, that was just what housed his eternal spirit, but then it was hard to make the distinction. In that moment of grief, it's hard to think like a Christian.

Eventually, Everyone Leaves

You know the more interesting part of these days, when all was said and done everyone left – went back home, went back to their lives, to their healthy children and we were left ALONE!

That is the one harsh reality with every loss; everyone eventually goes away, when the business goes broke, when the spouse passes on, when the divorce happens, when the sickness eats deeper and deeper.

At some point everyone leaves, they also have their

lives to live as much as they mean well and want to be with you always, there is always a point when you're alone with God, alone with your memories, alone to cry as much as you have tears to flow.

I went through moments when I literally felt my breath get cut imagining his lifelessness. There were emotions I felt which I could not describe.

All I could do was sing – "Tell me what can I do, 'cause I can't live without you, I can't live without you" by Tye Tribett. The only difference is that this time I was not singing for God but for my son. Living life without him looked so bleak.

At this point in my life, I did not even have a word or a scripture to encourage myself.

In reality, my life almost lost meaning; I seemed to be drowning in a pit of sorrow.

One day the Holy Spirit made me realise I was not the only one who had lost someone, "hubby had lost a dear son too, Nnoye, Dumebi and Debe had lost their sweet brother. How could I be so selfish in this sorrow?"

With this realisation, I dusted myself up and tried again to be a mother to the adorable children I had and be a wife to hubby once again.

> "But I would not have you to be ignorant, brethren, concerning them which are asleep, that ye sorrow not, even as others which have no hope"
>
> 1 Thessalonians 4: 13

All I lived for and still live for is to make sure the

separation is not forever. My life must make meaning for the kingdom of Christ so that at the end I will be re-united with my Justin in eternity.

With this resolution, I have made sure I try to maintain a regular prayer life and bible study. The question I still ask myself is "What is the sophisticated Christian way to mourn?"

I get very tearful and some days I really do not want to get out of bed. On other days I want to throw myself into work of any kind just to forget.

The one scripture I hated people reminding me of was;

> *"Blessed be the God and Father of mercies and God of all comfort, who comforts us in all our tribulation, that we may be able to comfort those who are in any trouble, with the comfort with which we ourselves are comforted by God."*
>
> *2 Corinthians 1: 3-4*

I would always ask, why I had to be the one to go through the experience so I can comfort others, but as Pastor Paul Adefarasin would remind us, while you ask "Why me?" also ask "Why not me?"

The one thing I learned though is that the words people speak will always fade away and it is truly only the God of all comfort that could come through for me in this time of sorrow.

I heard that the pain will ease; I don't know when because this pain I feel is so deep and so real, it looks like it is bottomless and has no end.

There are times when we have fond memories of

how we lived life with Justin but when the laughter is gone there are always tears.

The Hard Questions

In July 2016, unknown to me, my children embarked on a three-day fast, my husband had travelled back home at the time. This fast was done in such secrecy that I wondered what petition they were taking to God. I finally got someone to spill the beans – "We're praying for another baby brother".

This information broke my heart into a million pieces, first the fact that I was not in any way ready for another pregnancy, not at age 40.

Second reason was, I so want my children to see God as a loving Father that is interested in everything that concerns them and so He hears their prayers and will answer them. But will this be 'another' unanswered prayer from this loving God. I don't know. I figured to myself, if God made Justin by-pass the first family planning, then surely He can do it again, difference is that this time around I will not fight it. I will not however stop the family planning.

Of course, there were days when I really desired another baby, but I had to ask myself the critical questions:

Am I looking to replace Justin?

Will the next baby really be as cheerful and loving as Justin?

Will we be able to give that baby a fair chance at life

without comparing him/her with the last one?

Maybe I should adopt a child, but then again it definitely is not the same thing.

So right now, I am waiting on God my Father, knowing that He will heal the hearts of my children and bring them (and I) to a place where we really let go of the pain of Justin's death and have only fond memories each time we remember him.

10

My Letter to Justin

Justin Chuka my beloved son, I missed so many episodes of those programs you loved to watch because it was your dance time. Who would dance for me here my baby? We had to deal with giving away your stuff. Who really was worthy to get your clothes? Who?

We sent half of your things to Camp David and sent another half to Ingi's crèche. But hey, you know what? There are certain items we did not let go of, I still kept your wine coloured jacket which you loved to wear. That particular item I may keep with me forever.

With every baby dedication, it was hard to be excited for the new baby because I always remembered that I dedicated you at the same altar and you are no longer here with me.

*T*hat was my short note to my little Justin. At the time, it seemed that if I could 'speak' with him, it would dull the pain and make me heal faster.

However, that was not to be.

I went through seasons of being tearful whenever I saw a baby, any baby at all - even on TV. It was worse when I had to attend Baby Dedications at church. Oh, how it hurt so much.

Having to continue ministering to kids at church was another tall task, and I intentionally avoided Bible lessons such as "Jesus Raising Jairus' Daughter" because I could not genuinely teach the kids about Jesus raising any child from the dead when my own dead was not raised. Every day was painful. Somehow, I had to cope with ministering to these kids Sunday after Sunday, having to face them with the truth of the Gospel.

At first, I was mechanical about it just because I knew I had a responsibility towards these children, but more importantly, my driving force was the determination that none of these kids should be lost eternally. I remain determined that their souls will not be lost forever because their lives matter and their souls must be redeemed. No child should be eternally separated from their born-again parents. Justin's friends from church would also not be eternally separated from him. How awesome is that!

It's this same determination that gave birth to the outreaches we have annually. From the first memorial, it seemed wasteful to lay flowers at Justin's graveside because Justin is not in the grave anymore. I needed to do something that gave me a deeper connection with eternity. So we kicked off the outreach to minister to underprivileged kids living in squatter camps, a semi-legal area of town where those that cannot afford better accommodation setup homes built with wood and zinc.

We worked with a host within the Squatter Camps who helped us get about fifty kids with whom we would spend some hours sharing the gospel and teaching them new songs while providing a meal and snacks. We would then leave them with "goody bags" containing groceries for kids.

Having this annual outreach has helped to dull the pain. It's easier to look at a newborn and genuinely rejoice. I'm stronger now because I know that Justin is with his creator and the little I am doing here helps other kids in building a personal relationship with God.

> [14] But Jesus said, Suffer little children, and forbid them not, to come unto me: for of such is the kingdom of heaven
>
> *Matthew 19:14*

This scripture sums it all up for me. It's all about the little children. We can see a glimpse of heaven in their innocence.

If we learn to be like them, we will have a better relationship with the Father. Learn to be trusting like they are; just to believe that when God says He has got us, we know He has got us. Learn to be persistent like kids because when a child really wants something from you, they can ask you a million times until you respond positively. Learn to follow the voice of the father the way children do - The minute you go to fetch them and they hear your voice, they cling to you as though their lives depended on it. Learn to be grateful like they are because once you see the way they light up when they receive a gift from you, it's so amazing – can we learn to appreciate the Father this way?

There's so much to learn from these kids, and yes that's what, in memory of our darling Justin, takes me back to the Squatter Camps every year.

11

The Battle of Thoughts

*H*ere again, at this time in my life, God brought me right back to Job chapters 38 & 39 teaching me about his supremacy. There were arguments with friends and family trying to debunk the supremacy theory.

I was told it was the devil, I was told before the funeral to go back and speak to my son, take authority over his life and call him back to life, I was told all sorts. I was too weary to get angry with anyone.

"Why would you even insinuate in any way that I did not fight for the life of my son?" The thoughts came again.

In that hospital room I prayed, I cried, I begged, perhaps I gave up too soon. And yeah, even if it was the devil that touched my household are you saying God was not strong enough to stop the hand of the enemy?

Grief has a way of changing our character. Sometimes I find myself getting very angry, even over things that should not matter.

I have found my older daughter change over the past one year becoming a very angry teen, it may just be that she's entering the teen age faster than we thought but sometimes I also think she misses her brother so much she does not even know how to handle it.

For some weeks after he passed, she voiced the concern that he was left in her care when he ingested whatever it was that made him sick so it must have been her fault that he died. We tried hard to get that nonsense out of her head, I really pray and believe that we succeeded because she does not speak such words anymore.

My younger daughter went through the emotional trauma of thinking her baby brother did not like her before he passed and so she felt she needed a bit more time to be friends with him. This myth we also tried to debunk making her realise that Justin was such a kind soul and he loved every single member of his family deeply.

My Mom blamed herself for his death in her own way, claiming that perhaps if she had not come to South Africa on vacation the baby would not have died, so tell me, how come he did not die the first time she came visiting to take care of him?

So well, I found comfort in the supremacy of God.

The God who is in control of everything is also in control of my life. If he had wanted my baby to be snatched from the claws of death and returned to us alive and well that is exactly what would have happened.

There remains a purpose for all of this pain that I have had to deal with; there remains a bigger purpose for having a son I did not 'plan' for only to lose him very quickly. There yet remains a purpose much bigger than me. Pastor Jumoke has always told me that with time we will understand; so yeah I remained hopeful that with time I will really understand.

Really, when I think of the all-knowing God and the last few days of Justin I am a firm believer in God having a plan and a purpose for our lives.

Thursday 19th November 2015, Justin watched TV till 3am with grandma and for the first time on this her particular trip he did not sleep in the room with hubby and I, rather he went to grandma's room.

Friday morning, hubby went off to the clinic for an appointment, I got the other kids ready for school but felt too guilty about waking Justin up so I left him to sleep in with grandma and so by the time hubby got home and saw Justin he did not bother about going to work anymore, they spent a leisurely day together just being father and son.

All through that day in his own baby way he sang all the songs they were taught at the crèche ahead of the Christmas carol planned for some time in December. I was pleasantly shocked that he knew that many rhymes and Christmas songs and just as my people would say 'My money was working' I said same to myself.

I was so looking forward to attending the Christmas carol of 2015 just to watch him do his presentation. His white shirt, white shorts and Christmas hat had already been bought, waiting for the D-day.

12

Growing from Pain

Pain always grows – it can be beautiful or ugly but your pain will always grow. If we allow the growth to be negative, then the fruit of pain will be yet more pain but the fruit of pain can be great and beautiful. I now realise that the fruit of this growth has to be managed by us and determined by us.

It could either be the pain of a body being ravaged by sickness or disease; or the pain of a heart broken into a million bits by a love gone sour or in my situation, the pain from the loss of a loved one. Pain, if left unchecked, will eat deep into the soul. The more we hold on to this pain and caress it, the deeper it eats into us. There were days when I did not want to let go of the pain, it felt 'good' to think I was doing something to justify my loss – the puffy eyes, the lost look, the sorrow and everyone just wanting to say sorry.

It took me months to realise that the pain I was

nursing was not moving me forward, rather I was retrogressing.

Overcoming pain is not always an easy undertaking but it can be done. Thinking of my situation, there were some things that helped me manage more effectively.

Find a purpose

From the moment that I started working on the memorial outing to honour the memory of our dear Justin, the pain started to fade, the tears reduced and there was always a reason to wake up the next morning and the morning after that.

Purpose dulls the pain which life brings. With the days, weeks and months following the passing of Justin, I found myself better able to cope when I had something to look forward to and the days I decided to dwell on my baby I was beside myself.

Right now, Francis and I decided to spend a day at Camp David to mark Justin's memorial. Working on the project of spending a day with the under-privileged children at Camp David has given me a lot to look forward to. Just the thought of putting a smile on another child's face is something to look forward to.

Regarding purpose, it is also important to recognise that we cannot always confidently say we know what our purpose in life is, sometimes we really know, sometimes we just stumble upon it, sometimes it is thrust on us. However, the bottom line remains that each of us has a purpose and we have to seek it out.

> ²"*It is the glory of God to conceal a matter, But the glory of kings is to search out a matter*".

Proverbs 25: 2

Even when it is not so clear what our purpose is, it is our glory when we seek it out.

Remember you are not alone

The irony of life is the fact that somewhere out there; there is a mom that has lost her child like me and there is a child that has lost his/her mom. In the circle of life we must always do our best to put a smile on the next person's face.

Doing something for another child will initially be painful: For a long while it's been painful coming within one meter of a child that reminds me of Justin but it gets easier as the days go by.

Today, I can say that my pain has grown from tears into being a channel to put a smile on the next child's face. I don't know what tomorrow may bring but I pray that indeed the life of Justin will make more meaning even in death than in the short months that we were blessed to have him on this side of eternity.

Find strength through prayer

For me, my prayer closet was where I got the strength to go through my challenging season. My closet is where I exchange my weaknesses for God's strength. I even created a number of prayer points to help me get through and I will share them with you. You don't have to pray all of them at the same time. You can pick one a day, as from my experience; there are not many things you can talk to God about when you are going through deep pain.

It's been a gradual process I must say, because even more than a year later, I am still a total mess. I struggled initially to participate in the "*Pray For Boys*" series of The Watchers as I think that I should be praying for two sons and not just one son. I remember clearly back in 2015 when I first participated in the "*Pray For Boys*" series, oh I prayed for my boys – Justin and Debe. I specifically asked God to make clear to me the purpose of sending Justin into our lives, I dedicated many days just to pray into his future. I sometimes asked myself what did I gain? What really was the purpose of this young man Chukwuka Justin Olisa in our lives?

I don't have the answers yet, but I tell you I have found a place of safety in learning to pray week in week out with The Watchers. Learning to put aside my own pain and pray through with another sister living thousands of kilometres away from me who I have never met before. I am learning to seek solace in God's presence and as I break bread every week I realise that God paid the ultimate price by giving up His only son and so He surely understands the pain of giving up a son.

Yes, I am learning to pray and you should too. As Habakkuk 2: 1 says, "I will stand upon my watch, and set me upon the tower, and will watch to see what He will say unto me, and what I shall answer when I am reproved."

These are my prayer points:

1. *Lord, it hurts so much, I feel very lost right now. Please hold me in your arms and comfort me in a way that only you can. Help me get through today; help me take one day at a time. In Jesus mighty name. Amen.*

2. *Father, heal the heart of my children and make them strong. Help them to realise that you still love them much more than they can imagine. Send people to help them through this season and to be there for one another.*

3. *Lord, I don't know the reason why I am going through this pain; I need your grace to know what to do with this pain. What is the next step in my life? Restore me in more ways than one; restore my joy, my peace, my desire to live. Restore my trust in you.*

4. *Father, I acknowledge that nothing I go through has taken you by surprise, help me to understand this situation better. There is nothing that can stop you from being God, nothing can change who you are or strip you of your supremacy. Teach me to lean on the omnipotence of you.*

5. *Lord I decree and declare that affliction shall not arise a second time in my home. I shut the mouth of the grave and declare this far and no further. Never again will I bury another child (business or spouse). Never again will I have to go through*

such a season of great loss. The grave is defeated and we have victory over everything.

6. *Behold what manner of love the Father has bestowed on us that we should be called children of God. Lord, help me to understand how deep your love is even in this time that I feel cut off from you. Help me to receive an overflow of your love.*

7. *As I receive an overflow of your love, teach me to replicate the same in the lives of my amazing children.*

8. *Genesis 25:22 – But the children struggled together within her; and she said, "If all is well, why am I like this?" So she went to inquire of the Lord. Father, I know that the breakthrough has been conceived, but the struggle seems to be raging much more to climb out of this pit of despair and pain. Open my eyes oh Lord to know that the peace and joy that I have conceived will be carried full term and brought forth alive. No more miscarriage! No more still birth!*

9. *Lord, now when I feel so helpless and alone, help me to know that You are with me always, even when things seem tough, that you are right there by my side to bring me through to a place of glory.*

10. *Lord, I decree and declare that today marks a turnaround point in my life. All my dead dreams*

come alive once more. I declare that God is turning the pain I feel into abundance, affection and anointing.

11.   *Lord today I declare that it is time for me to stand up, make that decision to move on and not allow the pain of my past be a stronghold that stops me from accessing my glorious future.*

12.   *Father, I speak an end to every chronic condition in my life that has caused me pain. Help me realise that healing is a process, teach me to trust you dear God while I am in this process.*

Everyone feels pain for different reasons and at different times. I encourage you, don't let your pain dictate how the story ends, instead take that pain back to the master and let Him use it as a major ingredient in your future.